GOD SEES YOUR TEARS

30 PRAYERS FOR COMFORT AND HEALING

CAROLYN RICE

CONTENTS

Published by Alarias Press,

Po Box 248, Granite Falls WA 98252

Unless otherwise noted, all scripture verses are from the Holy Bible, New King James Version®, NKJV ®, Copyright © 1979, 1980, 1982 by Thomas Nelson, Inc., Publishers. Used by Permission.

This book is not intended as a substitute for the medical advice of physicians or psychologists. The reader should regularly consult a physician or psychologist in matters relating to his/her mental health and particularly with respect to any symptoms that may require diagnosis or medical attention.

INTRODUCTION

When you're going through trials, or just trying to heal from a past that doesn't seem to want to let you go, you can feel isolated and alone. At times you may feel as if no one in the world knows what you are going through, and even if you could talk about it, it may be hard to get the words out at all.

I felt this way more often than not as God took me through a time of healing from severe abuse. There were days I simply sat in His presence with tears running down my face. There was nothing I could say in that moment, yet God comforted me with His very presence.

This is my gift to you, a book of thirty prayers, all dealing with different topics I myself have dealt with, and the words that eventually came after I brought my tears to God.

In His love,
    Carolyn

JOURNEY OF HEALING

*D*ear Father God, this journey of healing begins and ends with you. For you are the Alpha and the Omega (See Revelation 22:13). As I take your hand, and you lead me on this journey, there will be those that aren't happy about it. There will be those who will try to stop me from healing. But there will also be those who will love and support me through times and seasons. Yet it will always begin and end with you.

When hard times come, help me not to give up. When people are not excited about my healing journey, or even try to stop it altogether, I pray you would give me the strength and courage to move forward, and not allow their agendas to hinder me. Let you be the one I want to please the most. Let you be the one I live and breathe for. Take all codependency, wrong roots and unhealthy patterns out of my life. In Jesus name, amen.

And let us not grow weary while doing good, for in due season we shall reap if we do not lose heart.

CAROLYN RICE

~

Galatians 6:9

TEARS

Thank you, Father God, that you have seen every tear I've ever cried. I've never been alone, for you are with you me. My tears are so precious to you that you have saved them in your bottle and written about them in your book. You know what each one was about. Tears of sorrow, tears of joy, tears of absolute desperation and heartache.

Thank you that your plan for me is restoration and healing. For every tear I've ever cried, I will reap a harvest, for your word says that those who sow in tears shall reap in joy (see Psalm 126:5).

I choose to trust you that you will bring restoration and healing to my life. These tears will not always be my story, but I declare that I shall testify of how you worked in my life during these times of tears. In Jesus name, amen.

Put my tears into Your bottle; Are they not in Your book?

~

Psalm 56:8

REJECTION

Father God, thank you that when you look at me, you see what Jesus did for me. I am covered by the blood of the lamb (See 1 Peter 1:19).

I declare out loud today, that I am accepted in the beloved, and loved by my Heavenly Father.

Lord, where rejection has hurt and wounded my soul, I pray you would bring healing. Help me to know that you look upon me with love and compassion in your eyes, and to know that love completely and wholly.

Walk me out of rejection and into the knowledge that I am loved completely and without hindrance.

In Jesus name, Amen.

To the praise of the glory of his grace, wherein he hath made us accepted in the beloved.

~

Ephesians 1:6 KJV

SHAME

Father God, where I have been made to feel shameful, or to feel that I was bad in some way, I ask for your healing. I pray that you would help me to see myself as you see me, beautiful, valuable, cherished and loved.

In the name of your Son Jesus Christ, I break the ropes of shame off me now, and I unbind them from me. I will not give shame a place in my life anymore. Father God, where a root of shame has grown in my life, I now apply the blood of Jesus Christ to that root, and I pray that you would destroy it. Shame, I renounce every agreement I have made with you, and I tell you to leave me now. I declare that I am loved and accepted by my heavenly Father, cleansed by the blood of the Lamb, and that I am made as white as snow.

Father God, where other people have done things to me, to make me feel ashamed, I choose to forgive them now, and surrender what they did into your hands. This does not mean they get away with it, but that I place them into your hands for you to deal with.

I pray you would bring healing to those places in my mind, emotions, body and spirit that were wounded and damaged by what someone else did. I choose to trust you for my healing. In Jesus name, amen.

Do not fear, for you will not be ashamed; Neither be disgraced, for you will not be put to shame; For you will forget the shame of your youth and will not remember the reproach of your widowhood anymore.

~

Isaiah 54:4

FEELING UGLY INSIDE

❧

*D*addy God, where this world made me feel ugly, unworthy and unloved, I ask for your restoration. Where my own sense of self has been shattered, I pray that you would pick up every piece and put me back together again in Christ.

I declare that I am beautiful and unashamed in the eyes of the King of all kings. I look up and I pray Father God, for your face to shine upon me, and give me peace (See Numbers 6:25-26). As I spend time with you in worship and prayer, bring healing to my soul.

In Jesus name, Amen.

And I put a jewel in your nose, earrings in your ears, and a beautiful crown on your head.

~

Ezekiel 16:12

WORDS

ather God, where I have been wounded by the words of others, I invite you in to begin the healing process. I choose to forgive _____ for speaking those ugly words, and I place _____ into your hands and surrender them to you, _____ is your burden and not mine.

In the name of Jesus Christ, I wipe away the ugly words that have been spoken about me in my hearing and out of my hearing. I renounce all agreements with those words made by me or anyone else, and I break their power to hurt me now. I declare that I am a child of God, and I agree with what my Heavenly Father says about me.

In Jesus name, Amen.

Death and life are in the power of the tongue

~

Proverbs 18:21

MIND

Father God, in the name of Jesus Christ I surrender my mind to you. I declare that I have the mind of Christ, and I plead the blood of Jesus over my mind. I break the assignments of the enemy over my mind now, in the name of Jesus Christ.

Father God, As I read your word, I pray that you would give me understanding and that your word would bring healing to my mind, for your word is alive and powerful (See Hebrews 4:12).

When I struggle with my thoughts, I pray that you would remind me of the truth of your word.

I declare peace over my mind.

In Jesus name, Amen.

You will keep him in perfect peace, whose mind is stayed on you, because he trusts in you.

~

Isaiah 26:3

EMOTIONS

ather God, when my emotions are raw and seem to be taking over, I cry out to you. I give you each one of my emotions, all the anger, sadness and fear, and I lift them into your hands. I invite you Father God, into my emotions.

Where emotions have held me captive to pain and sorrow from the past, I pray that you would unlock the door to the prison I have been kept in. Come in and give me the strength to step out. Bring me to a place where my emotions no longer rule me.

Lord, I want to walk in your peace. I choose to praise you in song and thank you for something every day.

I pray your healing balm over my emotions, and I invite your presence in to begin the healing process in me. In Jesus name, amen.

A time to weep, and a time to laugh; A time to mourn, and a time to dance

~

Ecclesiastes 3:4

HIS PLANS AND PURPOSES

ather God, I yield to you my own plans and purposes, and I ask you what your plans are for me.

I thank you that you will show me the next step to take. I also ask that you restore to me all the years that have been stolen (See Joel 2:25), and that you would repurpose them for your glory.

I lay down at your feet all agendas and expectations that others have placed upon me. I now take up your plans, and I thank you that your burden is light. I commit all my ways to you now, and I thank you that you will establish me in your will. Stir up the gifts you have placed in me and let them make room for me (See Proverbs 18:16). In Jesus name, amen.

For I know the thoughts that I think toward you, says the Lord,
thoughts of peace and not of evil, to give you a future and a hope.

~

Jeremiah 29:11

MEMORIES

*F*ather God, I bring every bad, harmful and scary memory to you. I place them at your feet now, and I invite you into those painful places.

Where the door has been closed, and those memories have been hidden in the darkness, I pray that in your gentle way, you bring your light to them. Help me know that I don't have to be afraid, that you're with me, and will never leave me nor forsake me (See Hebrews 13:5). Thank you, Father, that you have a plan for my restoration.

Lord, where these memories have haunted me, bring me to a place of healing. For you are the great healer, and I put my trust in you.

In Jesus name, amen.

Let not your heart be troubled; you believe in God, believe also in Me.

~

John 14:1

ANGER

ather God, I bring to you the anger I feel. Help me to release it in healthy ways. Father, you created me with emotions, and anger tells me that something is wrong. Help me to be angry and sin not. Show me healthy ways to release my anger.

In the name of Jesus, I repent for letting my anger lead me into any sin. And in the name of Jesus, you spirit of anger I break your hold on me. I renounce every agreement I have made with the spirit of anger, and you spirit of anger, I tell you to leave me now. You are no longer welcome here.

Thank you, Father God, for replacing my anger with peace and helping me to set healthy boundaries. Thank you that you will not leave me here. In Jesus name, amen

Be angry, and do not sin: do not let the sun go down on your wrath

~

Ephesians 4:26

OPPRESSION

⚜

*I*n the name of Jesus, no weapon formed against me will prosper (Isaiah 54:17). I forgive those who I have anything against, and I release them into God's hands. I renounce every agreement I have made with oppression now.

Father God, I pray in Jesus name that you would open a door for my freedom. I invite your presence into my life. Thank you that you have delivered me out of darkness and brought me into the kingdom of your dear Son. Strengthen me, and help me to keep standing for my spiritual, emotional and physical healing, and to never ever give up. In Jesus name, Amen.

He has delivered us from the power of darkness and conveyed us into the kingdom of the Son of His love

~

Colossians 1:13

DEPRESSION

*In the name of Jesus Christ, I remove this cloak of depression from me now. I choose to praise today.

I choose to think on the things I am thankful for.

I choose life.

I choose to believe that things will not always be this way, that God is in my corner, and I can trust Him.

I choose this next breath.

I choose to believe that weeping may last for a night, but joy comes in the morning (See Psalm 30:5).

Father God take this depression from me, I want to exchange it for your joy. Take this grief from me, I want to experience the joy of your presence.

I choose to walk in faith today, that depression is not the end of my story.

In Jesus name, Amen.

To console those who mourn in Zion, to give them beauty for ashes, the oil of joy for mourning, the garment of praise for the spirit of heaviness; That they may be called trees of righteousness, the planting of the Lord, that He may be glorified.

~

Isaiah 61:3

BROKEN HEART

*F*ather God, I lift my heart into your hands today, every broken piece. I thank you Father that nothing is wasted, but you will use this for the purpose of your kingdom. Lord, thank you that you have not forgotten about me. Breathe life back into my heart. Breathe life back into my spirit, and where brokenness has reigned, I invite you in to heal my heart. Help me to live again in the abundance of your joy. Where I can't even imagine being joyful, I ask for your presence to come and heal.

I choose to hope for a better day. I choose to believe your promises to me are true, and I choose to live with the faith that you are the healer of my broken heart, and that it will not always be this way. In Jesus name, Amen.

A bruised reed He will not break, and smoking flax He will not quench; He will bring forth justice for truth.

~

Isaiah 42:3

RESTORATION

I thank you Father God, that you have a plan for my restoration. I choose to align myself with your plans and to have godly boundaries with those who would try to keep me on the path of woundedness.

Lord, rebuild me from the ground up and make me new in you (See 2 Cor 5:17). I invite your Holy Spirit in to be my helper (See John 14:26), and I close all doors to the enemy now by the power and the name of Jesus Christ and His blood shed for me.

I thank you that your word is alive and active (See Heb 4:12), and that as I am in your word and in prayer, you will do a healing work in me. Thank you for directing my steps in the way I should go. In Jesus name, Amen

I will repay you for the years the locusts have eaten—
the great locust and the young locust,
the other locusts and the locust swarm

~

Joel 2:25

FEAR

*ather God, I pray for your courage today to face every fear that stands up against me. Help me to know that I am not alone when I am following you, and that you will never leave me nor forsake me (See Heb 13:5). I pray that your presence and your love would be manifest in my life, and that you would deliver me from every fear as I walk out my life with you. Help me to be strong and courageous in the face of fear. In the name of Jesus, amen.

I sought the Lord, and he answered me;
he delivered me from all my fears

~

Psalm 34:4 NIV

ANXIETY

nxiety, I do not agree with you anymore. I renounce every agreement I have made with you, and I choose to believe the promises of God rather than the lies you tell me about my outcome.

Father God, I ask you to bring your truth to my mind when I struggle with anxiety. Do not let anxiety win the battle over me but help me to walk with faith in your promises. Help me to know that I have a good Father on my side who is with me every moment. Pull out the root of anxiety in my life. In the name of Jesus, amen.

Do not be anxious about anything, but in every situation, by prayer and petition, with thanksgiving, present your requests to God.

~

Philippians 4:6 NIV

UNHEALTHY PATTERNS

ather God, I pray that you would go into my root system and prune unhealthy patterns and unhealthy ways from me. Where my growth has been stunted, I pray that you bring dead things back to life, and stunted growth into full growth.

Help me to receive your love for me, to have healthy boundaries, and to be full of your love for others and for myself. I want to be healthy Lord, body, mind and soul. I pray that you would breathe life back into me now, in Jesus name, amen.

Being confident of this very thing, that He who has begun a good work in you will complete it until the day of Jesus Christ;

~

Philippians 1:6

A PRAYER OF FORGIVENESS

ather God, I choose to forgive _____ for _____. I repent for holding this offense against _____. I choose to release _____ into your hands, he/she is not my burden anymore, but he/she is yours. Help me to have healthy boundaries with _____. I choose to trust you to give _____ what she/he needs.

I surrender my heart to you, and invite you in to heal, restore and refresh me physically, spiritually and emotionally. Help me not to hold on to this offense anymore. In Jesus name I pray, Amen.

And whenever you stand praying, if you have anything against anyone, forgive him, that your Father in heaven may also forgive you your trespasses.

~

Mark 11:25

PUT ON YOUR ARMOR

⁂

*I*n the name of Jesus, I put on my helmet of salvation, my breastplate of righteousness, my belt of truth and my shoes of the gospel of peace. I take up my shield of faith and my sword of the spirit in Jesus name. I plead the blood of Jesus over my mind, and I pray Father God that you would direct my steps today, into your plans and your will for my life. I surrender to you my hurts and wounds, and I give up all grudges and offense now. I choose to forgive. I choose to spend time with you today through prayer, and the word of God. I choose this day to follow you. Prepare me for what is ahead. In Jesus name, Amen.

Stand therefore, having girded your waist with truth, having put on the breastplate of righteousness, and having shod your feet with the preparation of the gospel of peace; above all, taking the shield of faith with which you will be able to quench all the fiery darts of the wicked one. And take the helmet of salvation, and the sword of the Spirit, which is the word of God;
~Ephesians 6:14-17

TRUST

❦

Father God, I want to trust you. When I am afraid, I ask that you fill me with courage and the knowledge that even when things look bleak, you will never leave me nor forsake me (See Deut. 31:8).

Thank you that your word says you are not a man that you should lie, and those things you have promised you will do.

Walk me out of distrust. Heal the places in me where experience has taught me not to trust. Help me believe that your promises are true, and that they are for me. Help me believe that you are for me and that you will do what you say you will. In Jesus name, Amen.

God is not a man, that He should lie,
Nor a son of man, that He should repent.
Has He said, and will He not do?
Or has He spoken, and will He not make it good?

~

Numbers 23:19

BREAKING MANIPULATION AND CONTROL

❦

Father God, I walk this earth right now because you have chosen me to be here. My purpose is in you alone.

Where others have tried to manipulate or malign me for their own purposes, I break those soul ties with _____ now, and I refuse to be manipulated any longer. You spirit of manipulation and control, I break your power over me, and I renounce every agreement I have made with you. Manipulation and control, I close the door on you. You are not welcome here anymore!

Daddy God, I pray that you would give me a wisdom and discernment, that where people would try to manipulate and control, I would notice right away and have the wisdom to know what you would have me do.

I choose to serve you and you only, and if someone comes to try and make me serve them and their purposes, maligning your purpose for me, I ask that you help me to have healthy boundaries. But I also ask, that those that would not repent would be removed from their place of influence in my life. In Jesus name, amen.

Am I now trying to win the approval of human beings, or of God?
Or am I trying to please people? If I were still trying to please people,
I would not be a servant of Christ. ~
Galatians 1:10 NIV

CHOSEN

Father God, I thank you that before I was formed in my mother's womb you knew me (See Jeremiah 1:5). Before I took a breath, you knew who I would be, what my name would be, and how many days I would walk this earth. You knew every step before I even took one, and you knew every word on my tongue before one of them came to be.

You chose me to be yours. I am not a burden to you, and I am not an accident. I was thought of and dreamed up by you, and when I came to be, you rejoiced that I was here. I am precious, and a delight to you. Lord, help me know that I am chosen (See 1 Peter 2:9), that I am valuable and that I am loved. In Jesus name, Amen.

Your eyes saw my substance, being yet unformed.
And in Your book they all were written, the days fashioned for me,
When as yet there were none of them

~

Psalm 139:16

NEVER ALONE

Dear Daddy God,

You are the Father I never had. When _____ wasn't there, you were. When _____ didn't pray for me, you yourself made intercession for me (See Hebrews 7:25).

When I was afraid, you brought me into your arms to comfort me (See Isaiah 51:12).

When I felt alone, you were there (See Matthew 26:11).

When I felt I wasn't protected, you are the one who shielded me (See Psalm 3:3).

You kept me from things that could have gone wrong and led me out of things that were.

You have held my hand through every trial, and when I couldn't stand on my own, you held me up (See Isaiah 41:10).

When I couldn't stop the tears, you caught each one in your bottle (See Psalm 56:8).

Thank you that I have never walked alone, and I never will. In Jesus name, amen.

Fear not, for I am with you;
Be not dismayed, for I am your God.
I will strengthen you,
Yes, I will help you,
I will uphold you with My righteous right hand

~

Isaiah 41:10

LIES

Daddy God, the liar comes, and he tells me that you don't love me. He tells me you don't care.

Daddy God, the liar comes and tells me that I am all alone, and that no one will ever help me.

But I know that this is a lie. And I do not accept it anymore!

The truth is, I am loved by my Daddy God. I am cared about so much that my Daddy God's eyes are on me every second. He loves me so much He can't keep his eyes off me. I am never alone, because the word says that my Daddy God will never leave me nor forsake me (See Deut. 31:6), and He is working even now (See John 5:17).

He helps me to walk out of the darkness, into the light of His love (See Colossians 1:13).

And in the name of Jesus, where those lies have meant to keep me captive, I break their power now. I renounce every agreement I have made with those lies and I cast them down to the ground in Jesus name, amen.

The thief does not come except to steal, and to kill, and to destroy. I have come that they may have life, and that they may have it more abundantly

~

John 10:10

NO WEAPON FORMED AGAINST ME
WILL PROSPER

*In the name of Jesus, I declare that no weapon formed against me will prosper, but every tongue that has risen against me will be condemned, for this is the heritage of the servants of the Lord, and my righteousness is from Him.

Father God, I choose to trust you and to always go back to your word, and always stay close to you (See Psalm 119). I thank you that you will carry me through this, and that this is not the end of my story.

Help me to know that I will come out of this stronger than before, because you strengthen me. I find my peace and my hope in you. In Jesus name, amen.

No weapon formed against you shall prosper, and every tongue which rises against you in judgment You shall condemn. This is the heritage of the servants of the Lord, and their righteousness is from Me," Says the Lord

~

Isaiah 54:17

INSECURITY

*F*ather God, I surrender every insecurity I have struggled with to you. Thank you that you are not angry with me but have compassion and want to help me overcome them.

Lord, I pray that you would give me a confidence in who I am in you, and that insecurity would not hold me back anymore. Remove all of its hindrances from my life and help me to move forward without it.

Help me to know that you created me for a specific purpose, and everything I am fits perfectly, like a puzzle piece, for that purpose. But help me to also know, that I am first and foremost, your daughter.

I ask that you fill me with the certainty that no matter what anyone else thinks or says, I am loved by my heavenly Father, and you will never stop loving me. In Jesus name, Amen.

For we are His workmanship, created in Christ Jesus for good works,
which God prepared beforehand that we should walk in them.
~ Ephesians 2:10

CONDEMNATION

❧

*J*esus, I ask your forgiveness for
_____, and I thank you that
when I confess my sins to you, you are faithful
and just to forgive me of my sins and to cleanse me from
all unrighteousness. I receive your forgiveness and declare
that I am forgiven through the Blood of Jesus Christ. I
break the lies of the enemy off my mind, and I break off
all shame concerning this, in Jesus name.

I thank you Father God that the truth is You are
faithful and just to forgive me and cleanse me from all
unrighteousness. You paid for that sin on the cross for me. I
accept your gift of forgiveness, please heal me from all
condemnation. In Jesus name, amen.

*If we confess our sins, He is faithful and just to forgive us our sins
and to cleanse us from all unrighteousness*

~

1 John 1:9

UNWORTHINESS

*esus, thank you that you yourself have made me worthy by your blood. Your blood washed away my sin and made me white as snow. Your Blood gave me the gift of being able to come into the presence of the Father when I accepted you as my savior (See Hebrews 10:19). Your Blood paid for my sins and granted me eternal life.

As I fill my mind with your truth, wash the lies of unworthiness away and show me how much I am truly loved and cherished by you. I ask that you heal the memories and places in my heart that were injured and give root to the lie of unworthiness. In the name of Jesus, amen.

Come now, and let us reason together," Says the Lord, "Though your sins are like scarlet, they shall be as white as snow; Though they are red like crimson, they shall be as wool

~

Isaiah 1:18

THE REST OF THE JOURNEY

*esus, for the last thirty days I have asked you into different places in my heart and life that need healing. And now, I ask that you continue your healing for the remainder of my days. Lead me in the ways you have called me to go. As I read your word, bring comfort, healing and direction to my life. As I pray, speak to my heart, and as I walk with you, do a healing work in my life.

Take the things that have happened to me and redeem them for your purposes. Use what was meant for evil and turn it for good. Continue your restoration in my life and make it count for your kingdom. Help me to grow and mature in you. In Jesus name, amen.

who comforts us in all our tribulation, that we may be able to comfort those who are in any trouble, with the comfort with which we ourselves are comforted by God

~

2 Corinthians 1:4

JOIN CAROLYN'S NEWSLETTER

To receive updates on new books and author news, join Carolyn's newsletter at CarolynsBooks.com

OTHER BOOKS BY CAROLYN

Lord, Help Me Forgive: An 8 Week Journey Through
Forgiveness

Lord, Heal My Heart: A Devotional

Loved by the Father: A Women's Bible Study and Journal
through John and 1 John.

DID YOU LOVE THIS BOOK?

Please leave a review on Amazon, Barnes and Noble or Goodreads

ABOUT THE AUTHOR

Carolyn Rice holds an Associate Degree from Seattle Bible College. She has served in women's ministry, Alpha Ministries, home group ministry, prayer ministry and taught Cleansing Stream Seminars.

She has two grown children and a granddaughter, and lives with her husband and two Boxer dogs in Granite Falls, Washington.

Find out more about Carolyn and her books at Carolynsbooks.com.

www.ingramcontent.com/pod-product-compliance
Lightning Source LLC
Chambersburg PA
CBHW032028040426
42448CB00006B/763